DEDICATION

This book is dedicated to my wonderful parents who gave me a childhood full of great memories, lots of love, and heaps of fun!

Table of Contents

2 Games

- 3 The Psychiatrist
- 5 Mafia
- 9 Telephone
- 10 Truth or Dare
- 11 Would You Rather
- 12 Freeze Dance
- 13 Duck Duck Goose
- 14 Musical Pillow Pets
- 15 20 Questions
- 16 Guess the Song
- 17 Activity Horse
- 18 4 People and a Couch
- 20 Salad Bowl Charades
- 22 Charades Telephone
- 23 2 Truths and a Lie
- 24 Slap Circle
- 25 Never Have I Ever
- 26 Pterodactyl
- 27 Board Games
- 28 Card Games

29 Poga

35 Music

- 36 Dance Party
- 37 Performance Competition
- 38 Karaoke Session

39 Recipes

- 40 Scotcheroos
- 41 Peanut Butter Pie
- 42 Pizza Biscuits
- 43 Oreo Truffles
- 44 Buckeyes
- 45 Cracker Sandwiches
- 46 Brownie Batter Dip

47 Photo Spot

Games

Games are the heart and soul of every sleepover. With so many fantastic options, everyone is guaranteed to have a blast. Flip through the following pages to discover the ultimate guide to the best sleepover games ever!

The Psychiatrist	Guess the Song
Mafia	Activity Horse
Telephone	4 People and a Couch
Truth or Dare	Salad Bowl Charades
Would You Rather	Charades Telephone
Freeze Dance	2 Truths and a Lie
Duck Duck Goose	Slap Circle
Musical Pillow Pets	Never Have I Ever
20 Questions	Pterodactyl

THE PSYCHIATRIST

The Psychiatrist is a game that involves skill, a little thinking, and a lot of laughs. It's perfect for any size party, with guests of all ages. It's customizable, and can bring out that secret silly side of any person.

Set Up

One person is deemed "the psychiatrist".

"The psychiatrist" will step away and relocate somewhere they can't see or hear what the rest of the group is doing or saying.

The rest of the group will sit in a circle, leaving a spot for "the psychiatrist" to return.

How to Play

♡ The rest of the group will come up with a "pattern".

♡ "The psychiatrist" will return and join the circle.

♡ Starting with any player, "the psychiatrist" will take turns asking any sort of question, in which that player will have to answer in the form of the "pattern".

♡ The psychiatrist will in turn guess the pattern.

The Pattern

The pattern can be anything from the spelling of the words used in an answer, to body language, to themes.

To make it more competitive, you can keep track of how many questions it takes for "the psychiatrist" to guess the pattern. Whoever guesses in the least amount of questions is the winner.

Some examples can include:

♥ Answers must start with the letter "Q". This can lead to some pretty silly answers and a lot of laughs.

♥ Everyone will touch their leg after answering the question. Tip: the more subtly you do it, the harder it is to guess!

ABABA

> **Bringing to Mars**
>
> This is an another version of the game that you might have heard of. In this version, the "astronaut" is the only one who comes up with the pattern, and each player goes around in circles and and asks "can I bring xyz" to Mars.

Once "the psychiatrist" has guessed the pattern, the game is over!

MAFIA

Mafia is a game best played with a lot of people! The more people, the better. Full of twists and turns, this game brings out friendly (or maybe not so friendly) rivalries and competition. The better you can lie, the better you will do!

Set Up

The easiest way to set up this game is with a deck of cards. First, take out 2 aces, 1 king, and 1 queen. Set aside. Next, count out the total number of people playing the game. You will need one less card than the amount of people. The 4 cards already taken out are a part of the total.

> For example: if there are 10 people playing, the total amount of cards will be 9. You already have of the cards (the 2 aces, 1 king, and 1 queen). You still need 5 more cards. In this case, you will take out 5 random number cards from the deck to use as fillers for the "townspeople".

Someone is designated as the "narrator". This person will know what is going on from each perspective of the game. They are "all knowing", and come up with the stories for each round. This person will hand out the cards face down. Each person may look at their own card, but may not share it with any other player.

Make sure each player knows what role they will play.

How to Play

Each round consists of everyone going to "sleep" (closing their eyes). The narrator will ask the mafia to "wake up", which indicates to the players that received the ace cards to open their eyes.

The narrator will ask them to choose who they want to "kill". As inconspicuously as possible, the two mafia will agree on who they want to be out the rest of the game. The narrator will then ask them to close their eyes.

The narrator will the ask the detective to wake up. The player who had received the king card will open their eyes. The narrator will ask who they think the mafia is. The detective will point to someone, and the narrator will shake their head yes or no depending on if they are a part of the mafia or not (no lying!)

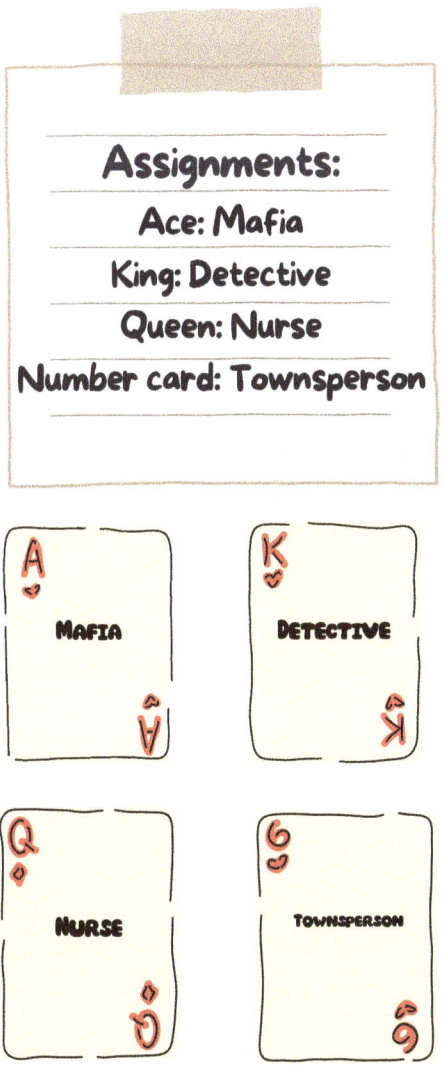

The narrator will then ask the nurse to wake up. The player who received the queen card will open their eyes. The narrator will ask who they want to save. The nurse will point to someone that they believe might have been targeted by the mafia. The narrator will then ask them to close their eyes.

The narrator then asks everyone to wake up, and relays the story to everyone.

Whoever the mafia killed off is now out of the game and cannot participate in the conversations; however, they can keep their eyes open the whole time now; unless the nurse saved them! In this case the narrator will explain how a murder was attempted on said player, and that they were saved.

Then comes the arguing, voting, and chaos! Everyone must decide who they think might be a part of the mafia. If no one can agree on the same player, then a vote is taken and whoever has the most votes is "killed off", and is also out of the game.

The rounds continue until either the mafia is the last one standing (only one has to survive), or if the townspeople kill off both mafia.

Example story: "People of Transylvania, wake up! Last night, Clara was out getting dinner and a bat came out of nowhere and sucked her blood, and she died. Who do we think did it?"

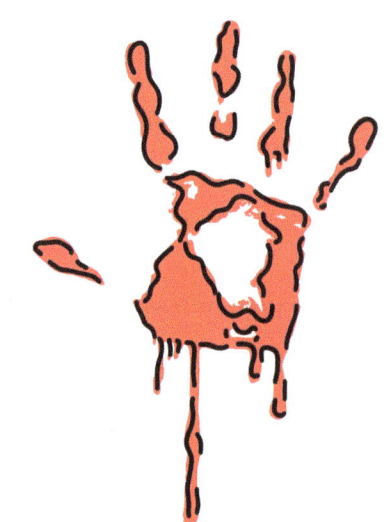

Ways to change it up:

Pick a location! If everyone picks a certain location, the stories can become even more wild and entertaining each round.

Add more mafia! If there are more than 15 players, you can add more mafia to keep the game going even longer.

Variations

Murder: This game is a simpler version. In this version, someone must sit out in order to pick the "murderer". Everyone closes their eyes, and the person who sits out taps one player. This signals to them that they are the murderer. Next, everyone sits in a circle. One person is chosen to go in the middle. They must continually swivel their head around and try to figure out who the murderer is. The murderer will (try to) wait until the middle player is looking away; once this happens, they make eye contact with another player and stick their tongue out. That player then has 5 seconds to die dramatically. This keeps going until the middle player guesses or everyone dies but the murderer. The middle player gets 2 guesses until they lose.

Vampire: Similar to murder, this game has someone as the vampire/murderer. This time, everyone walks around aimlessly like a zombie, with someone as the detective. The vampire will bare their teeth inconspicuously to someone as they pass, and that person has 5 seconds to dramatically die. The detective must solve who the vampire is.

Telephone

Telephone is easily one of the most simple, yet entertaining games that has been around for a long time. It's perfect for any amount of people at any age!

Set Up

Players must sit in some sort of circle/line.

How to Play

The player at the beginning of the line or circle will think of a phrase they want to say. They will then whisper it to the next player, who then continues this process until it reaches the end. The last player will repeat the phrase aloud. The phrase might have stayed the same, or might be totally off!

Truth or Dare is a game that you may have heard of, or may have even played! Just remember to keep it safe and inclusive, and everyone will have fun!

TRUTH OR DARE

This game is very casual. Players just need to sit close together so they can be within talking distance.

Each player will get to pick whether they want to honestly answer a question (truth) or complete a task chosen by other players (dare). Once they pick one, they must stick with their choice. If they decide they don't want to answer or don't want to do the challenge, they lose!

Examples of "Truth" Questions:
Who is your celebrity crush?
What is your guilty pleasure?
What is your most embarassing moment?

Examples of "Dares":
I dare you to lick your toe.
I dare you to prank call your uncle.
I dare you to sing.

WOULD YOU RATHER

Would You Rather is an all inclusive game for any age, ability, and skill. It can get those giggles going, and those wheels turning.

Each player takes a turn. The other players will come up with a "this or that" question, essentially picking two different scenarios, and asking which one the player would pick.

> The best type of questions are the silly or the extreme questions.

Examples

Would you rather eat only pickles for the rest of your life or only have pickles for fingers for the rest of your life?

Would you rather be stuck in an elevator with wet dogs or have to go sledding with a wet dog?

 FREEZE DANCE

This is a game GREAT for any age, especially the ones who have the wiggles!

All you need is a way to play music, and a designated DJ.

Everyone will gather in one area. The DJ will play a song, and everyone will start dancing. The DJ will choose to stop the song whenever they want. All players MUST stop dancing as soon as the music stops. Whether they are on one leg, hands in the air, or on the ground, everyone must freeze right where they are! If a player can't hold their pose, or is still dancing when the music stops, they are out.

This continues until one player is left standing.

DUCK DUCK GOOSE

This classic, interactive game gets everyone excited to see who will get picked next. The suspense leads to surprises, laughs, and tons of fun.

All players must sit in a circle on the floor. One player is designated the "ducker". This person will stand up and walk around while tapping each player on the head and saying "duck". The player will continue this until they decide to pick one player, in which they will tap on their head and say "goose". The "goose" will jump up and start chasing the "ducker" around the circle. The ducker must make it back to the goose's spot without getting caught by the goose.

If they get caught by the goose, they must sit in the middle for the next round.

The object of this game is to have fun!

MUSICAL PILLOW PETS

Have you heard of musical chairs? Then you know how to play musical pillow pets! The best part about it is you can have all your sleepover guests bring their own pillow pet for this game, which brings in fun variety.

Set Up

Someone needs to be designated as the DJ. This person will control the music. The rest of the players will be the "walkers". Count up the number of walkers and subtract one. This is the number of pillow pets you need.

How to Play

Set up the pillow pets in a circle. Have the walkers stand around the pillow pets in a circle. The DJ will start the music and the players will walk in a clockwise circle around the pillow pets. Once the DJ stops the music, the walkers must find a pillow pet to sit on. Because there is one less pillow pet, someone will not get one. This player is then out.

For the next round, one pillow pet must be removed. Then you repeat the same steps of playing the music and walking in a circle.

The last person standing is the winner.

20 QUESTIONS

This game is ideal for when you've gotten all your wiggles out, and you need a relaxing activity before bedtime.

One person will think of something- literally anything: an object, a place, an emotion. Then, this person will say what category their "thing" falls in.

✦ ★ ✦ ★ ✦ ★ ✦ ★ ✦ ★ ✦ ★ ✦

For example: if the player is thinking of spaghetti, their category could be food.

✦ ★ ✦ ★ ✦ ★ ✦ ★ ✦ ★ ✦ ★ ✦

The other players will then ask yes or no questions. But be careful, they only get 20 total! So think before you ask. If the other players are able to guess the object by the 20th question, they win. If they are unable to guess it, the player who thought of the original object wins!

Tip: to make it harder, you can eliminate the category, and just have the other players start guessing.

GUESS THE SONG

What's the best way to test everyone's ear for music? By having them guess all your favorite songs!

How to Play:

Someone will be the DJ for the round. This person will use a phone, or some other device to play songs. They will play the first 5 seconds and see if any other player can guess the song. If no one can guess the song, then the DJ will play another 5 seconds... and so on, and so forth, until a player is able to guess the song.

CCCC

Variations
Instead of playing the song from a device, the DJ can:
- Whistle the song
- Hum the song
- Mouth the song

ACTIVITY HORSE

If you have ever played Horse in basketball, this is very similar, but with a fun twist!

How to Play

- Set an order in which players will go.
- The first player will do a "trick". This can be an acrobatic move, something embarrassing, or anything you can think of.
- The next players will go in the order. If they are unable to (or do not want to) do the challenge, they receive an "H".
- Once each player has gone, the next player in the order gets to do their "trick".
- This continues on, and if a player already has an "H", they will receive an "O", then an "R", and so on until the word horse is spelled. Once someone has a "horse", they are out.

You can use any word you want!

4 PEOPLE & A COUCH

This game works best with large groups, and creates the best kind of chaos and fun! It can take a while to finish, but it's a blast and the time will fly by.

Set Up

 Each player gets a small piece of paper to write their name on.

 The group then gets split up into 2 teams. This can be done anyway you choose, but it's easier to remember when it's something visible, such as hair color.

 Every player needs a seat, plus one extra. There must be a set of 4 chairs in a row (preferably a 4 seater couch) that is designated as the winning spots. The winning seats start out split between the teams.

How to Play

⭐ Everyone is sitting in a circle.

⭐ The player with an empty seat to their right starts.

⭐ They will call out the name of someone in the room.

⭐ This person will get up and move to the empty seat.

⭐ Those players then switch pieces of paper, essentially switching names.

⭐ The next person with an empty seat to their right then calls out a name, and that person will move.

⭐ The catch is that people will start having different names, and so you won't remember who is who and who is where.

⭐ An empty seat on the "couch" means another chance for a player from one team to get a winning spot.

This continues until one team has all the winning spots.

Start:
Team 1   Team 2   Team 1   Team 2

Finish:
Team 1   Team 1   Team 1   Team 1

SALAD BOWL CHARADES

If you have ever played regular charades, you are one step ahead of the game!

Set Up

Each player will write a Charades item on a piece of paper. All pieces of paper will go into a bowl- shake 'em up like a salad!

You can either play a friendly round with no teams, or divide into 2 teams.

There will be three rounds.

1 The first round will be the easiest; this is the round where everyone gets to know the different items on the paper. The first player will take out an item, and a timer of 30 seconds will be set. The player has 30 seconds to verbally describe their item to the team. If the team can guess within the 30 seconds, they get a point. This continues around the circle until everyone has gone.

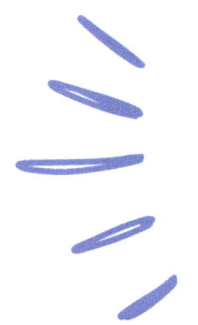 

Once the first round is complete, all players throw their papers back into the bowl. The "salad" gets tossed again!

2 The second round runs the same as the first, except this round uses the rules of regular charades. The player must act out their card as opposed to describing it. Again, a 30 second timer is set and if the team can guess it then they receive a point.

3 The third round is going to be the hardest. Repeat the process of putting the paper back and shaking it up. This time, as you go around the circle, the player gets to use 1 word to describe their item. Hopefully everyone has gotten to know the different options, and will be able to pick out which one it is. Again, a 30 second timer is set.

Whichever team has the most points at the end wins!

CHARADES TELEPHONE

Get ready for a lively twist on regular charades that will have everyone moving and laughing with unstoppable giggles and cackles.

Set Up

Everyone lines up, all facing the back of the player in front of them. The player at the back of the line starts.

How to Play

This player will think of a fun dance move, a silly pose, or something similar. Then they will have the player in front of them turn around. They will execute the movement. The new player will try to execute the movement for the next player, and so on. At the end, all the players will be able to see if the movement stayed the same or if it changed by the end of the line.

> 2 Truths and a Lie is the perfect ice breaker game. It's a great activity for when guests don't know each other and it's a fun way to uncover surprising facts about everyone!
>
> # 2 TRUTHS & A LIE

Each player takes a turn. They will come up with 3 facts about themselves; 2 of the facts will be true, and 1 will be a lie.

Once these are stated, the other players will discuss and see if they can figure out what the lie is.

• •

Although there is a technical winner, this game is meant to be played to help others get to know each other, and it is usually more fun without a competition aspect. But feel free to add in that the other players win if they guess the lie on their first guess!

• •

SLAP CIRCLE

A fun and interactive game for any age, this is a hit at any group gathering. It brings about lots of silliness, excitement, and laughs.

Set Up:

This game requires a bit of a different set up. All players must get into a circle on their bellies. Everyone's arms will end up being crossed with the player to each side. Essentially, each player will cross their right arm over the players arm to their left.

You can also play this game up on a table if some aren't able to get down to the floor.

How to Play:

The game consists of slapping either once or twice. Slapping once leads to the player with the hand next in line to slap once, and so on. If someone slaps twice, the slaps get reversed. The challenge is that your arms are not right in front of you; this leads to people slapping in the wrong order, the wrong arm, or not slapping at all.
if you mess up, you are out and must step out of the circle!

The last 2 players left are the winners!

NEVER HAVE I EVER

Never Have I Ever is a great way to help guests get to know one another, and is perfect for those late night secret sharing sessions!

Set Up This game is great because it requires minimal set up! All you need is players to be sitting in close proximity (something similar to a circle).

How to Play Each player puts their fists out in front of them. One player will start by saying something that they have never done, but they think other people in the group have done.

If another player has indeed done this activity, the player will put a finger up.

This continues, with each player saying something they have never done.

When someone has all 10 fingers up, they are out!

Never have I ever eaten sushi.

The object of the game is to be the last player in the game.

Tip: Think of activities you think a lot of other players have done, but that you have not. This will help ensure a lot of other players put their finger up on your turn.

PTERODACTYL

Set Up:

Players must sit in a circle.

How to Play:

Someone starts by saying "pterodactyl" to the next player. This continues on in a circle until someone wants to switch directions. In this case, they would turn the other way and make a pterodactyl noise.

The catch? You must not show your teeth at all. You must use your lips to cover your bottom and top teeth. If you show your teeth at any point whether it's laughing, cracking a smile, or your mouth starts to hurt, you're out!

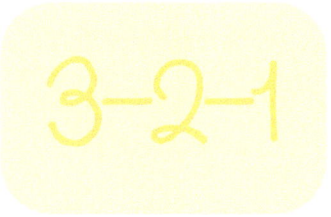

3-2-1 is a game that's great for a smaller group of friends who are in the mood for mayhem and wild connections.

Set Up

Players can decide to either all go at once or go around the circle.

If everyone is going at the same time:

- Everyone thinks of a random object- literally any object in existence.
- Someone counts down from 3. Then all players will shout out their word at the same time.
- Everyone must then think of a word that connects all the words together.
- Again, someone counts down from 3. Then all players will shout out their word at the same time.
- This continues on, and hopefully the words will relate more and more.

The game is over when all players shout out the same word at the same time.

> Example:
> If the first two words said are "baby" and "cheese", a word that could relate these is "milk", as babies drink milk, and milk and cheese are both a type of dairy.

If players are going around the circle:

- The first 2 players (player A and player B) will think of any object- any object in existence ever.
- Someone counts down from 3. Player A and player B will shout out their word at the same time.
- Then, player B and the player to the right of player B (player C) will think of a word that connects the first 2 words.
- Again, someone counts down from 3. Then player B and C will shout their word at the same time.
- This continues on, and hopefully the words will relate more and more.

The game is over when any 2 players shout the same word.

> The game works the same with only 2 players. The two players will take the role of all the players and just continue relating the words until they get to the same word.

The object of the game is for players to reach the same word.

Board Games

Here is a list of the best board games to have ready to go!

- Quelf
- Headbandz
- Secret Hitler
- Pandemic
- Catan
- Clue
- Trivial Pursuit
- Codenames

- Operation
- Sushi Go
- Villianous
- Ticket to Ride
- Monopoly
- Telestrations
- Twister
- Pie Face

- Life
- Trouble
- Azul
- Quirkle
- Herd Mentality
- Taboo
- Resistance
- Uno

CARD GAMES

Here is a list of great card games to bring out! Some of them require only a deck of cards, and some of them require a special deck.

- ♠ B.S.
- ♠ Egyptian Rat Slap
- ♠ The Great Dalmuti
- ♠ Rummy
- ♠ Spoons
- ♠ Go Fish
- ♠ Golf
- ♠ Apples to Apples
- ♠ Gin Rummy
- ♠ Euchre
- ♠ Hearts
- ♠ Kings in the Corner
- ♠ Nertz
- ♠ Uno
- ♠ Exploding Kittens
- ♠ Monopoly Deal

Poga

Partner Yoga

Poga, otherwise known as partner yoga, is an interactive way to incorporate talent, adventure, and fun without leaving the comfort of your basement.

Rules before starting:

 Always make sure you make the area around you safe. Add padding such as blankets, pillows, or tumbling mats underneath you so if you happen to fall, you have a safe place to land.

 Only attempt a particular poga pose if you are certain that you and your partners are physically able to do the trick. If something seems too difficult, try an easier pose instead.

 Always check with an adult before attempting any poga.

Each pose is labeled with a difficulty rating: 1 being easy, and 5 being very difficult.

Difficulty: 3

UPWARD SWAN

Difficulty: 5

THE FAN

Difficulty: 5

TRIPLED TABLE

Difficulty: 3

THE STACK

Difficulty: 5

THE PYRAMID

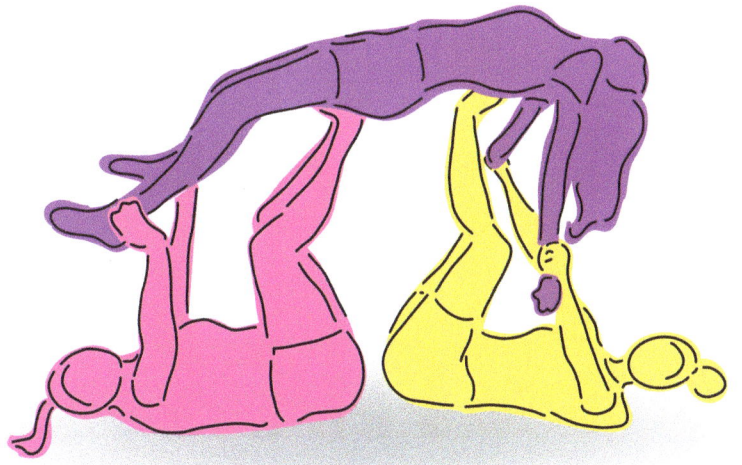

Difficulty: 2

HUMAN SACRIFICE

Difficulty: 4

QUAD STACK

Difficulty: 2

AIRPLANE

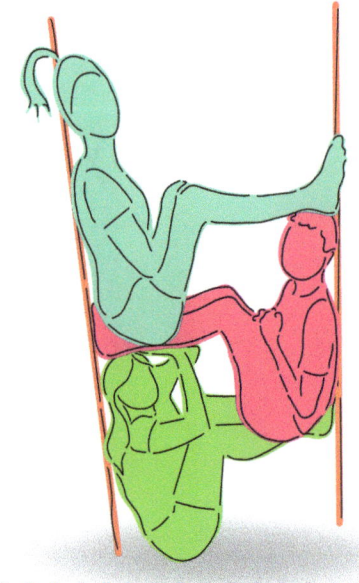

Difficulty: 4

DOOR STACK

Difficulty: 2

DIGGING DOG

Difficulty: 3

STANDING PYRAMID

Difficulty: 2

INVERTED PYRAMID

MUSIC

Music is an essential part of ANY party, sleepover, or get together.

The following pages have different and fun ways to incorporate music, singing, and dancing into a sleepover.

Performance Competition

Dance Party Time

Karaoke Session

Performance Competition

What's better than a late night dance party with a little competition and choreography? Nothing!

There are multiple ways to organize a performance competition. Guests can pick a partner or divide into small groups. Next, each group chooses their own song, or collectively everyone chooses the same song. Each group will go off somewhere and spend 30 minutes to an hour choreographing their dance/performance. Once the time is up, everyone meets back and shows off what they have been working on!

List of Songs (just to get you started: be creative and think of any song you want!)

Wannabe - Spice Girls
Peanut Butter Jelly - Galantis
Nobody's Perfect - Hannah Montana
Baby - Justin Bieber
Party in the USA - Miley Cyrus
California Gurls - Katy Perry
Classic - MTKO
Jump in the Line - Harry Belafonte
Rockin Robin - Bobby Day
We Go Together - Grease

Sh-Boom - The Chords
Walking on Sunshine - Katrina and the Waves
Fergalicious - Fergie
The Git Up - Blanco Brown
I Don't Dance - High School Musical 2
Lollipop - MIKA
Texas Hold 'Em - Beyonce
Hot To Go - Chapelle Roan
Don't Stop Me Now - Queen
121 - A Goofy Movie

Dance Party time

Some classic dance party songs that you can queue up for when you need to get that groove on!

Cha Cha Slide - DJ Casper
Cupid Shuffle - Cupid
Cotton Eyed Joe - Rednex
Hoedown Throwdown - Miley Cyrus
Cruisin' for a Bruisin' - Teen Beach Movie
We're All in This Together - High School Musical
The Git Up - Blanco Brown
Electric Slide - Marcia Griffiths
I2I - A Goofy Movie
Footloose - Kenny Loggins
YMCA - Village People
Hot To Go - Chapelle Roan
Time Warp - The Rocky Horror Picture Show
Gangnam Style - PSY

Bye Bye Bye - NSYNC
Party in the USA - Miley Cyrus
Don't Stop Me Now - Queen
Twist and Shout - The Beatles
Shake It Off - Taylor Swift
U Can't Touch This - MC Hammer
Dance the Night Away - Dua Lipa
Macarena - Los Del Mar
The Locomotion - Kylie Minoque
Uptown Funk - Mark Ronson
Watch Me (Whip/Nae Nae) - Silentó
The Hokey Pokey - Ram Trio
Old Town Road - Lil Nas X
Turbo Hustle - DJ Maestro

Karaoke

Sometimes all you need is some loud singing and some great friends. Karaoke is the best way to kick start those vocals! If you don't have a fancy karaoke machine, never fear! You can always pull up YouTube with the lyrics and use something silly for microphones. Here are some perfect songs for any karaoke night:

- We Don't Talk About Bruno - Encanto
- Call Me Maybe - Carly Rae Jepsen
- Single Ladies - Beyonce
- Our Song - Taylor Swift
- Mm Bop - Hanson
- Baby Shark - Hope Segoine
- Let It Go - Frozen
- I See The Light - Tangled
- Don't Stop Believin' - Journey
- Firework - Katy Perry
- We Will Rock You - Queen
- Man! I Feel Like A Woman - Shania Twain
- Can't Stop the Feelin - Justin Timberlake
- A Million Dreams - The Greatest Showman
- Dance Monkey - Tones and I
- Boomerang - Jojo Siwa
- Hakuna Matata - The Lion King
- Do You Want to Build A Snowman - Frozen
- Driver's License (Clean Version) - Olivia Rodrigo
- Happy - Pharrell Williams
- How Far I'll Go - Moana
- Unwritten - Natasha Bedingfield
- Girls Just Wanna Have Fun - Cyndi Lauper
- Ain't No Mountain High Enough - Marvin Gaye and Tammi Terrell

Recipes

Last but not least- you need yummies! The next few pages offer some amazing recipes to try for your next sleepover; whether it's salty, sweet, or somewhere in between.

Scotcheroos

Peanut Butter Pie

Pizza Biscuits

Oreo Truffles

Buckeyes

Cracker Sandwiches

Brownie Batter Dip

Scotcheroos

INGREDIENTS:

6 cups of rice cereal
1 cup of light corn syrup
1 cup of sugar
1 cup of peanut butter
1 cup of semi sweet choc. chips
1 cup of butterscotch choc. chips

Instructions:

1. Grab a large saucepan. Add in the sugar and the corn syrup, and set the heat to medium. Once it starts boiling and the sugar is dissolved, remove the pan from the heat.

2. Once removed from the heat, stir the peanut butter into the saucepan.

3. Put the rice cereal into a large bowl. Pour the sugar and peanut butter mixture over top and mix with a rubber spatula until well coated. Add the coated cereal to a sprayed 9x13 inch pan.

4. Melt chocolate chips and butterscotch chips together into a bowl. You can do this by placing them in a bowl and putting them in the microwave for 15 second increments and stirring in between.

5. Pour the chocolate mixture on top of the cereal mixture. Put the pan in the fridge and allow them to cool. You will know they are ready when the chocolate topping is hard to the touch.

Make these the night before the party!

Peanut Butter Pie

Ingredients:

1 cup of peanut butter
8 oz of softened cream cheese
9 inch graham cracker pie crust
1 1/4 cups of powdered sugar
1 container of whipped topping

Instructions:

Using a hand mixer, beat the cream cheese and peanut butter in a large bowl until fully combined.

Gradually add the powdered sugar and beat until fully combined.

Gently fold in the whipped topping.

Pour the mixture into the pie crust and place in the fridge overnight.

Make these the night before the party!

Pizza Biscuits

Ingredients:

2 cans of refrigerated biscuit dough
1 cup of shredded mozzerella
1/2 cup of pizza sauce

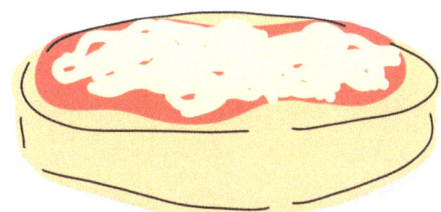

Instructions:

Take the biscuits out of the cans and lay flat on a sprayed cookie sheet.

Add 1-2 tbs of pizza sauce to each dough biscuit.

Add shredded cheese until the biscuit is mostly covered.

Cook the biscuits according to the package, but add one minute.

Oreo Truffles

Ingredients:

36 original oreos
8 oz of softened cream cheese
1 cup of semi sweet chocolate chips
1 tsp of vegetable shortening

Instructions:

- Place all 36 Oreos into a food processor. Pulse until they are crumbed.
- Add cream cheese and pulse again until fully combined.
- Scoop out small balls of the mixture and place on a parchment paper lined cookie sheet. Place the cookie sheet in the freezer for 20 minutes.
- Add the chocolate chips and shortening into a bowl. Microwave in 15 second intervals, mixing in between, until fully melted.
- Remove the cookie balls from the freezer. Using a toothpick, stick each ball into the melted chocolate.
- Place balls back into the fridge until the chocolate is hard to the touch.

Buckeyes

Ingredients:

1 stick of unsalted butter (softened)
2 cups of peanut butter
2 cups of semi sweet choc. chips
3 1/4 cups of powdered sugar
1/8 cup of brown sugar
1 tsp of vegetable shortening
1/4 tsp of salt
1 1/2 tsp vanilla

Instructions:

Pull out a stand mixer. Add the peanut butter and butter and mix on medium/high speed until fully combined. Add in brown sugar, vanilla, and salt. Mix together.

Gradually add in the powdered sugar. Make sure the mixer is turned off each time more sugar is added.

Roll the dough into balls and add to a cookie sheet. Place the cookie sheet in the freezer for 20 minutes.

Add the chocolate chips and shortening into a bowl and microwave in 15 second intervals until fully melted. Stir in between each interval.

Pull the balls out of the freezer. Use a toothpick to pick up the ball, and dip it into the chocolate mixture.

Place balls back in the fridge until the chocolate has hardened.

Cracker Sandwiches

Ingredients:

1 sleeve of round crackers
sliced deli ham
sliced American cheese
mustard
2 tbs melted butter

Instructions:

- Preheat your oven to 350 F.
- Get out a 9x13 casserole dish, and spray with cooking spray.
- Spread a layer of mustard on each cracker. Add meat to half of the crackers. Add cheese on top of the meat. Add another cracker on the top of each stack.
- Arrange all the crackers in a single layer in the casserole dish.
- Brush the top of all the crackers with the melted butter.
- Bake for 15 minutes.

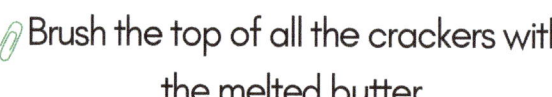

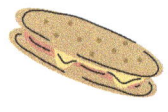

Enjoy the crackers!

Brownie Batter Dip

Ingredients:

8oz of softened cream cheese
1 container of whipped topping
1 box of brownie mix
2 tbs of milk
1 cup of mini semi sweet chocolate chips

Instructions:

Using a hand mixer, beat the cream cheese until it is smooth.

Using a rubber spatula, fold in the whipped topping until combined.

Add in the dry brownie mix and the milk, and beat until fully combined.

Fold in the chocolate chips.

Grab your dippers and dip!

Dippers:

- Grahamcrackers
- Marshmallows
- Pretzels
- Strawberries
- Wafercookies
- Animalcookies

MEMORIES

Tape sleepover photo here

Tape sleepover photo here